PIANO · VOCAL · GUITAR

CASTING CROWNS

UNTIL THE WHOLE WORLD HEARS

ISBN 978-1-4234-9010-4

HAL·LEONARD®
CORPORATION
7777 W. BLUEMOUND RD. P.O. BOX 13819 MILWAUKEE, WI 53213

Visit Hal Leonard Online at
www.halleonard.com

UNTIL THE WHOLE WORLD HEARS

Words and Music by MARK HALL,
ROGER GLIDEWELL, JASON McARTHUR
and BERNIE HERMS

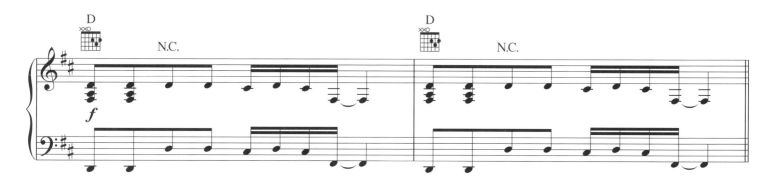

Lord, I want to feel with Your heart_____ and see the world thru Your eyes._____

* *Recorded a half step lower.*

I want to be Your hands and feet, _____ I want to live a life that leads. _____

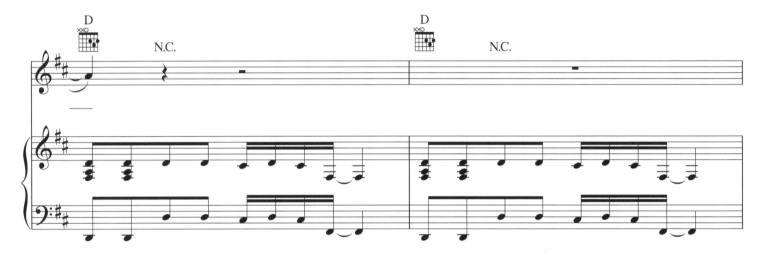

Read - y your - selves, read - y your - selves. _____ Let us

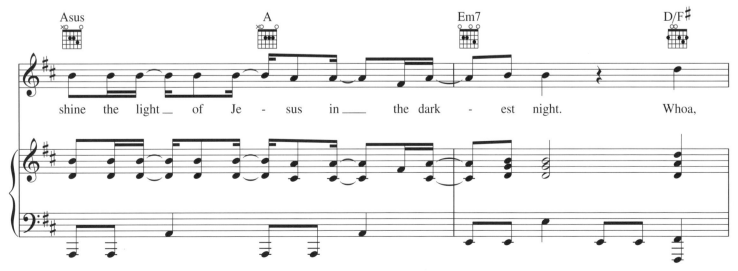

shine the light _ of Je - sus in _____ the dark - est night. Whoa,

voic - es in __ the wil - der - ness, __ we're cry - ing out. And as the

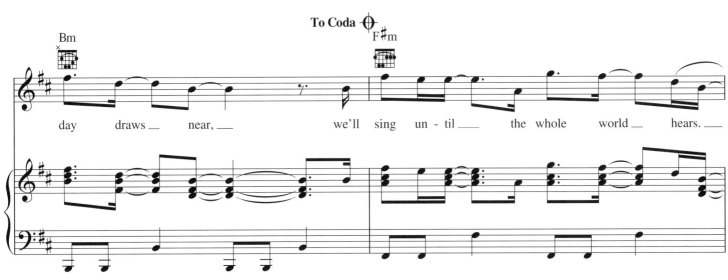

day draws __ near, __ we'll sing un - til __ the whole world __ hears. __

__ Lord,

let Your sleep - ing gi - ant rise, __ catch the de - mons by sur - prise. __

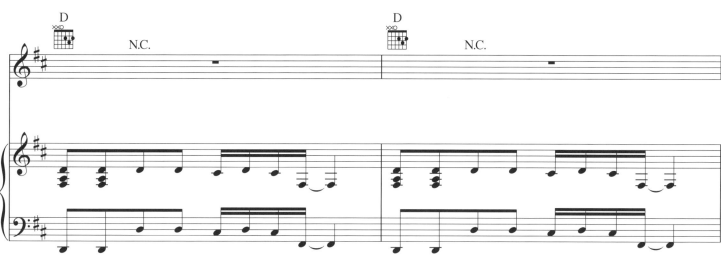

Ho - ly na - tions sanc - ti - fy, ___ let this be ___ our bat - tle cry. ___

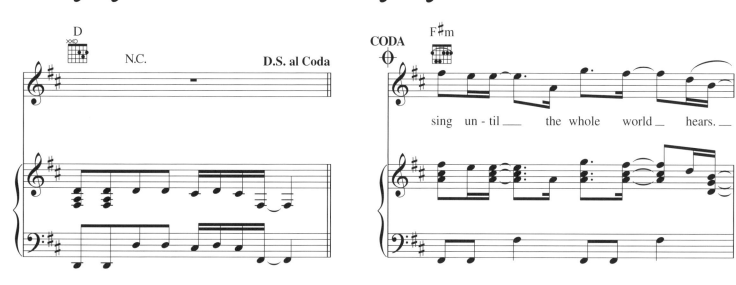

N.C.   **D.S. al Coda**   **CODA**

sing un - til ___ the whole world ___ hears. ___

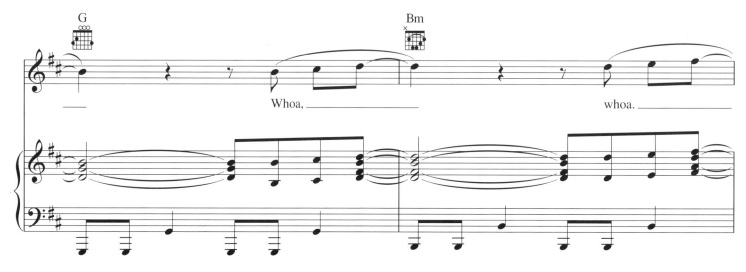

___   Whoa, _____   whoa. ___

We'll sing un-til ___ the whole world ___ hears. ___

Whoa, _____ whoa. _____

We'll sing un-til ___ the whole world ___ hears. ___

I want to be Your hands and feet, I want to live a life that leads,

to see You set the cap - tive free, _____ un - til the whole world _ hears. _

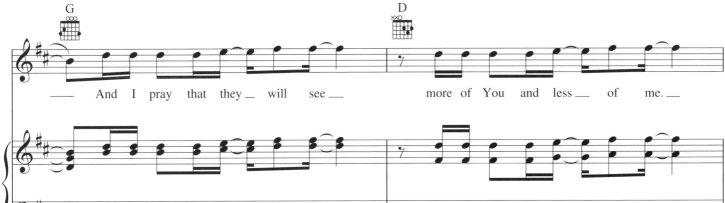

_ And I pray that they _ will see _ more of You and less _ of me. _

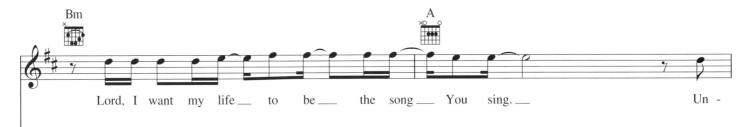

Lord, I want my life _ to be _ the song _ You sing. _ Un -

til the whole _ world hears, _ Lord, we are call - ing out,

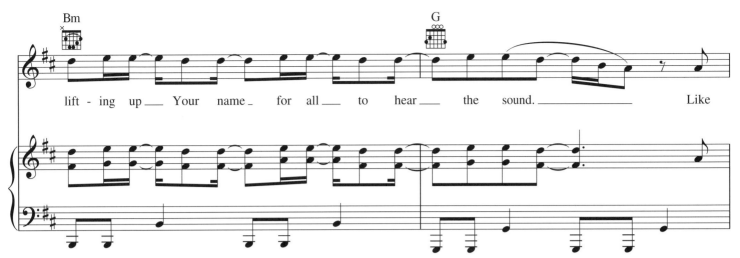

lift - ing up___ Your name___ for all___ to hear___ the sound._____ Like

voic - es in___ the wil - der - ness,___ we're cry - ing out.___ And as the

day draws___ near,___ we'll sing un - til___ the whole world___ hears.___

Whoa,_____ whoa._____

We'll sing un-til the whole world hears.

Whoa, whoa.

Repeat and Fade

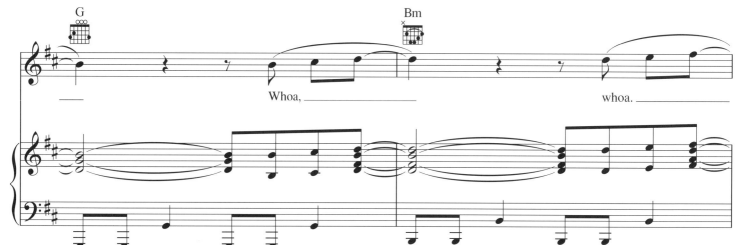

We'll sing un-til the whole world hears.

Optional Ending

sing un-til the whole world hears.

IF WE'VE EVER NEEDED YOU

Words and Music by MARK HALL
and BERNIE HERMS

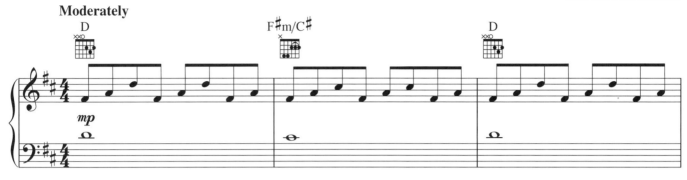

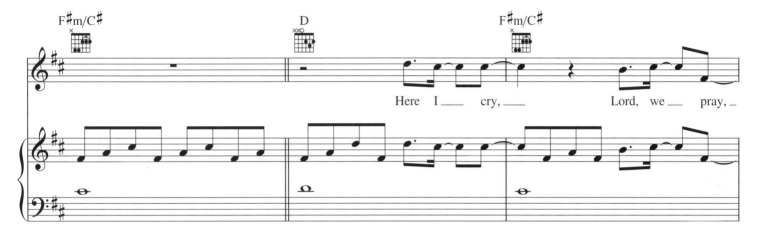

Here I __ cry, __ Lord, we __ pray, __

__ our fac-es __ down, __ our hands are __ raised. __ You called us __ out, __

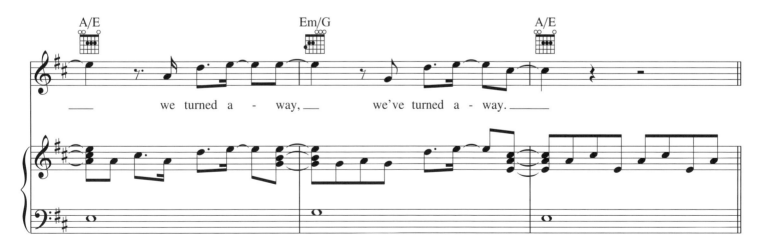

__ we turned a - way, __ we've turned a - way. __

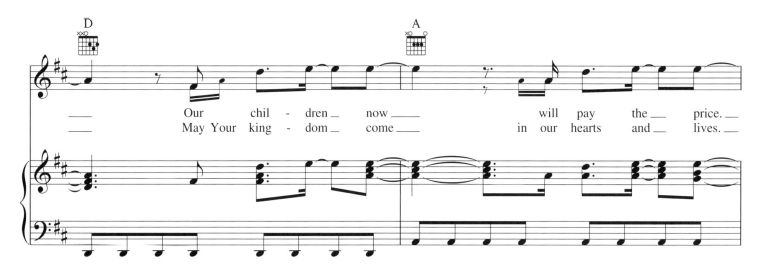

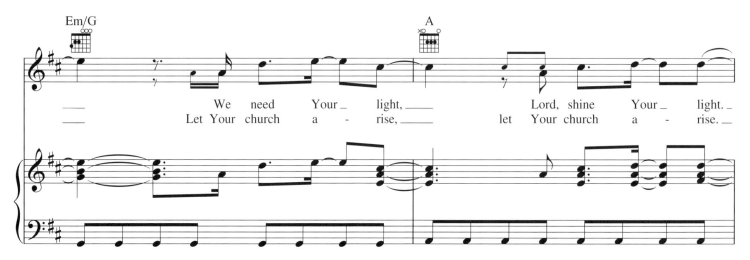

If we've ev-er need - ed ____ You, ____ Lord, __ it's __
__ now, ____ Lord, __ it's _____ now.

We are des-p'rate for ___ Your ____ hand. We're reach - ing out. __

We're reach - ing out. _____

We're reach - ing out.

We're reach - ing out.

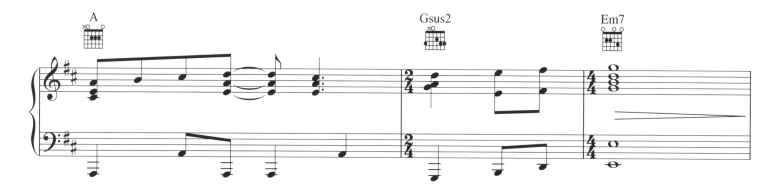

If we've ev - er need - ed You, Lord, it's

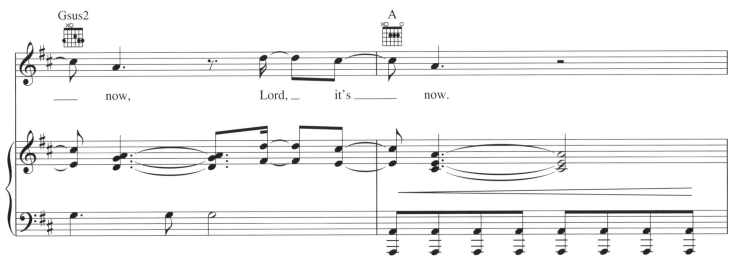

now, Lord, __ it's ___ now.

We are des - p'rate for Your ___ hand. We're reach - ing out. __

__ We're reach - ing out. ___

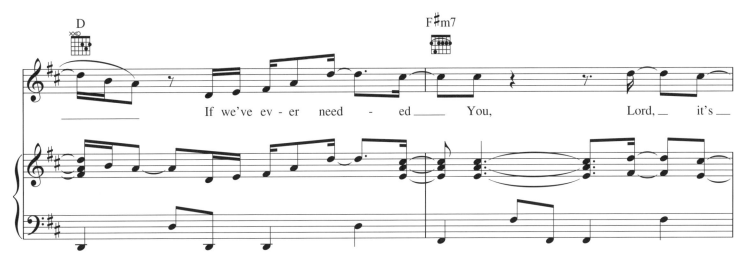

If we've ev - er need - ed ___ You, Lord, __ it's __

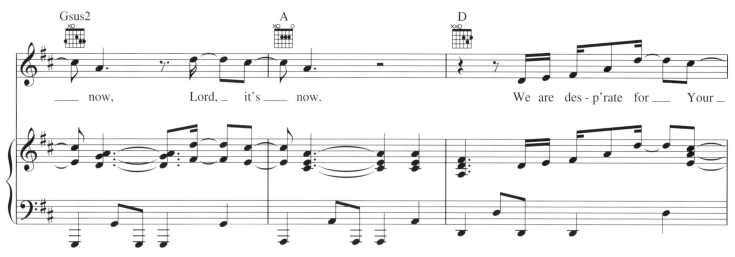

now, Lord, __ it's __ now. We are des - p'rate for __ Your __

__ hand. We're reach - ing out. __ We're reach - ing out. __

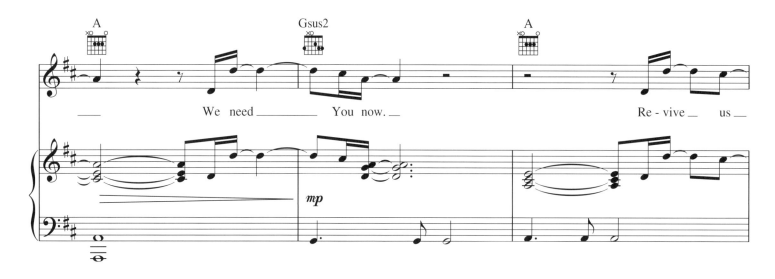

__ We need __ You now. __ Re - vive __ us __

__ now. We need __ You now. __

ALWAYS ENOUGH

Words and Music by MARK HALL,
ED CASH and MATT ARMSTRONG

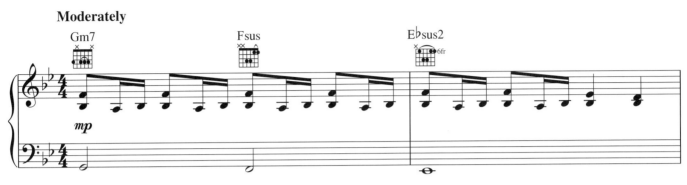

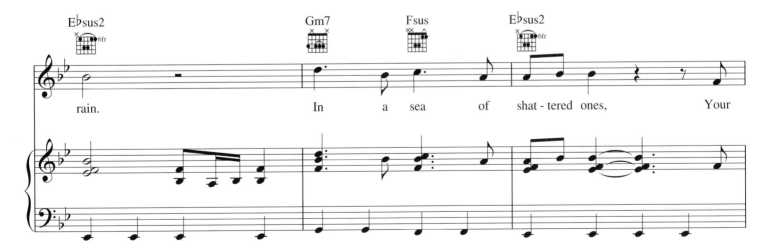

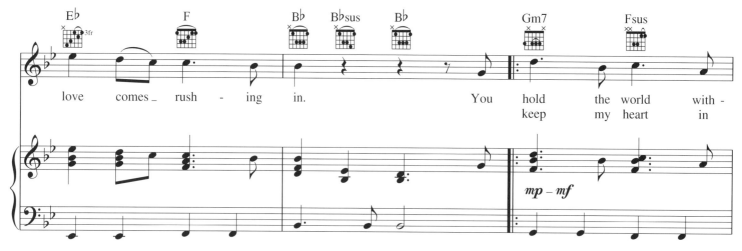

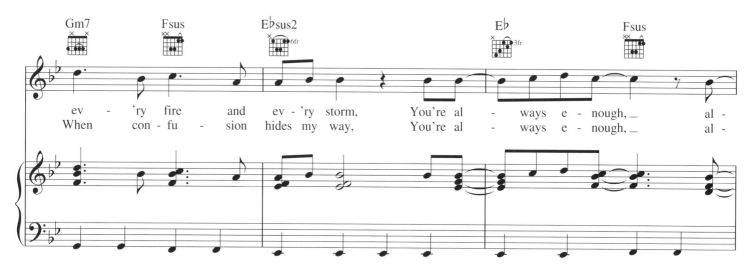

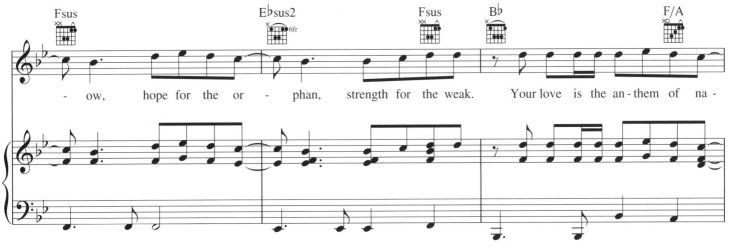

-ow, hope for the or-phan, strength for the weak. Your love is the an-them of na-

-tions, rings out through the ag - es, and You're al - ways e-nough__ for me.__

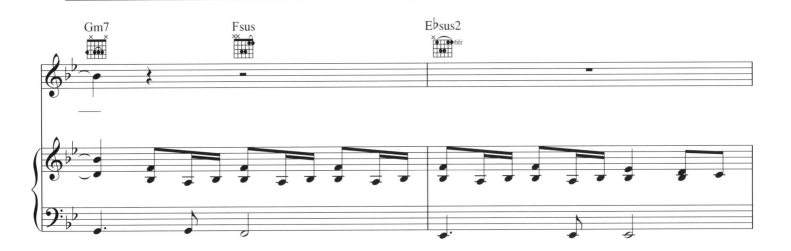

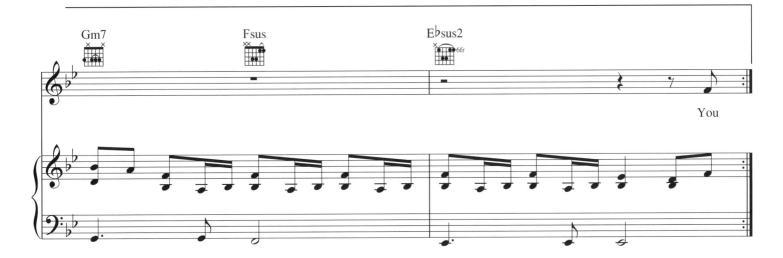

You

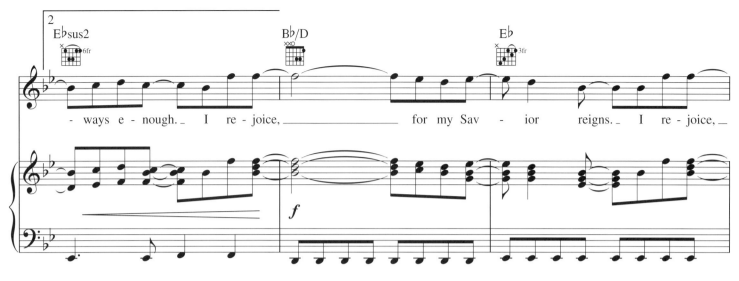

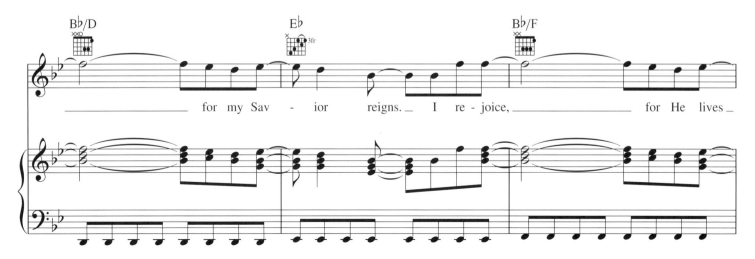

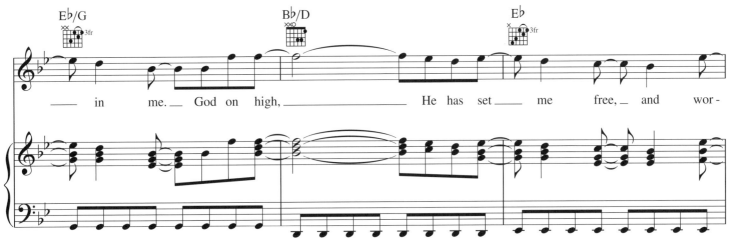

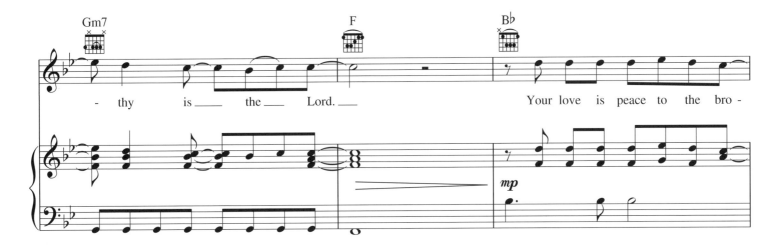

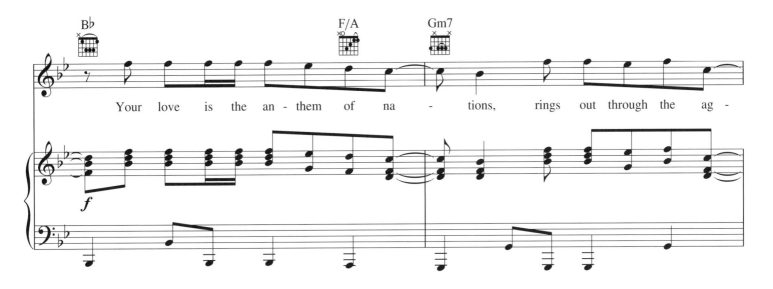

24

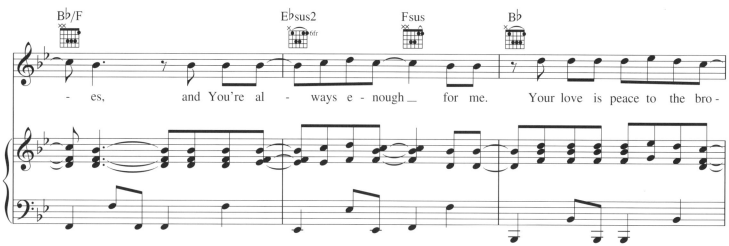

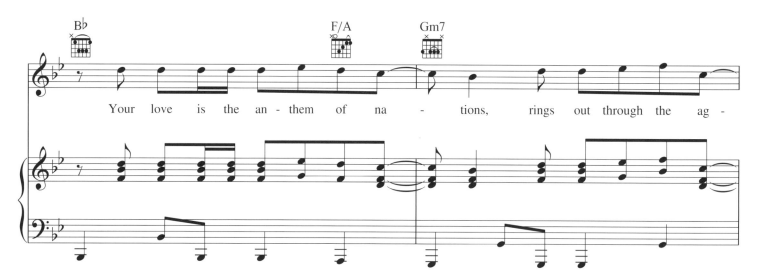

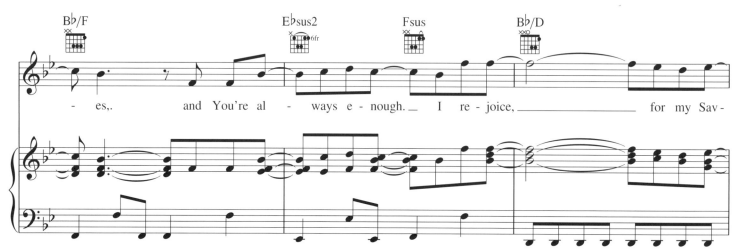

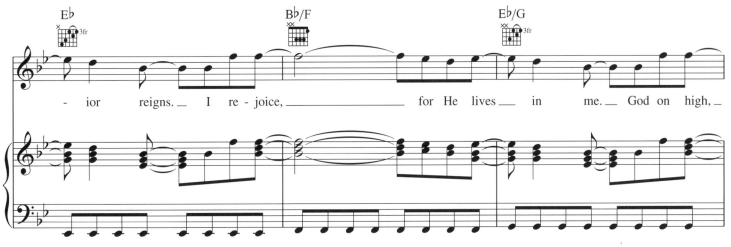

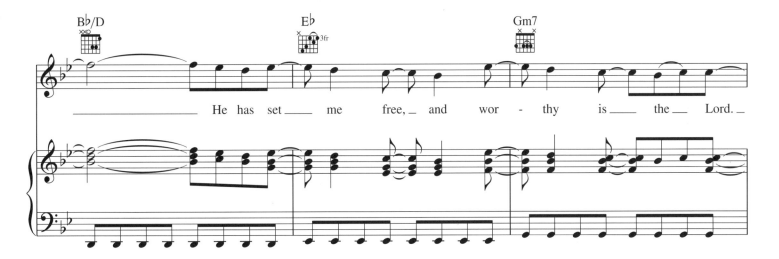

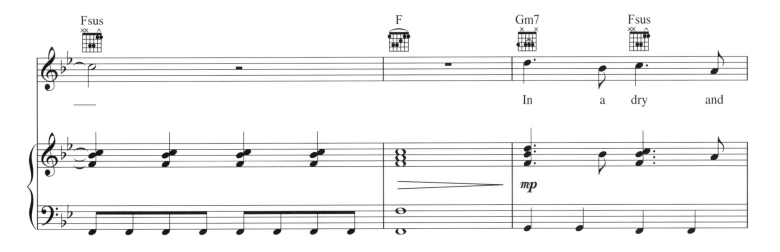

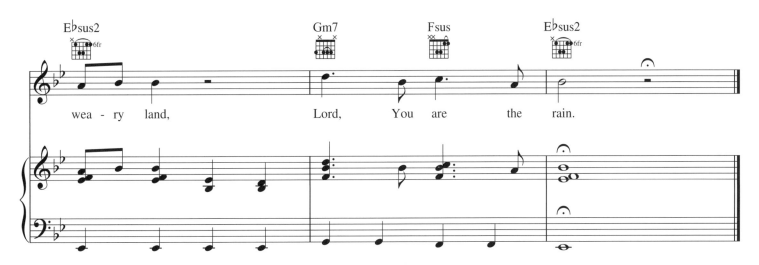

JOYFUL, JOYFUL

Words and Music by MARK HALL
and BERNIE HERMS

With excitement

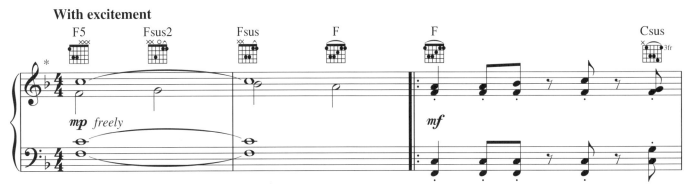

* Recorded a half step higher.

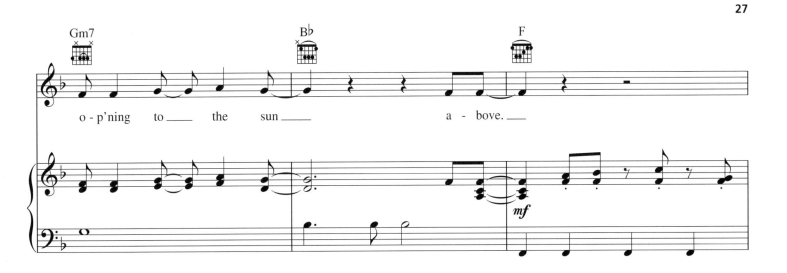

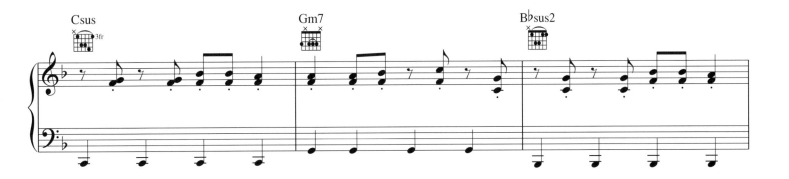

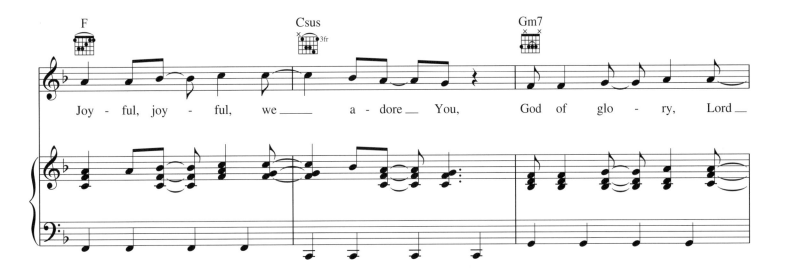

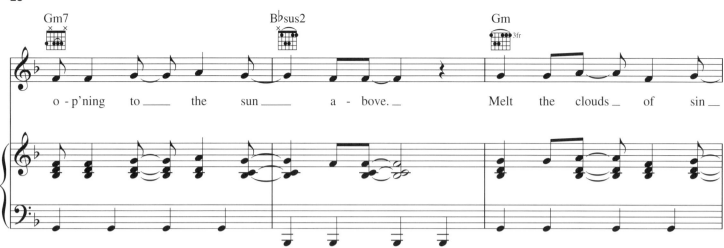

o-p'ning to ___ the sun ___ a - bove. ___ Melt the clouds ___ of sin ___

___ and sad - ness, drive the dark ___ of doubt ___ a - way. ___

Joy - ful, joy - ful we ___ a - dore ___ You. ___

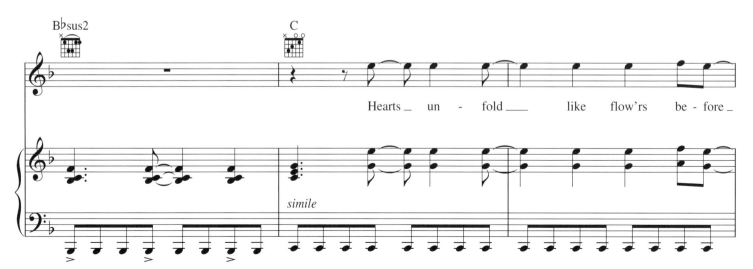

Hearts ___ un - fold ___ like flow'rs be - fore ___

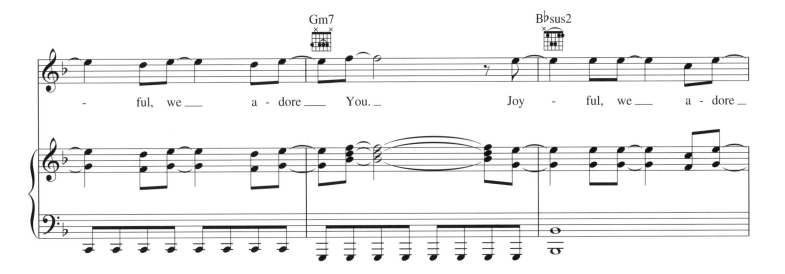

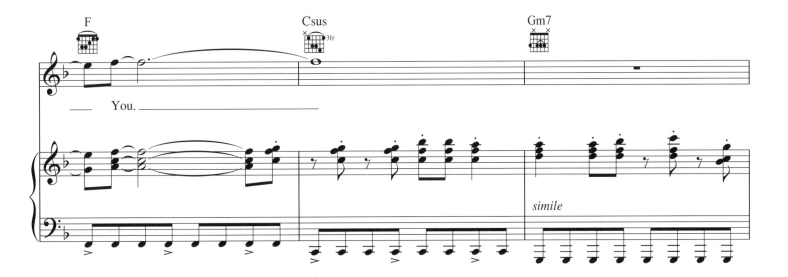

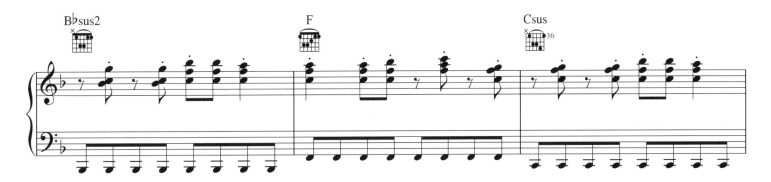

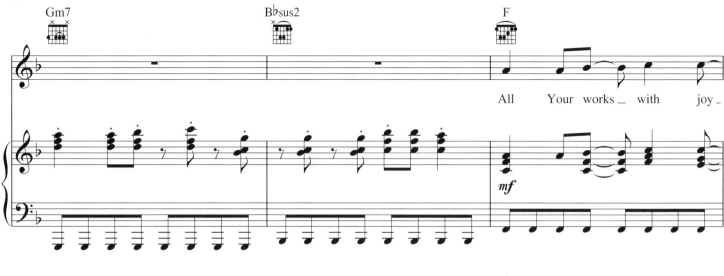

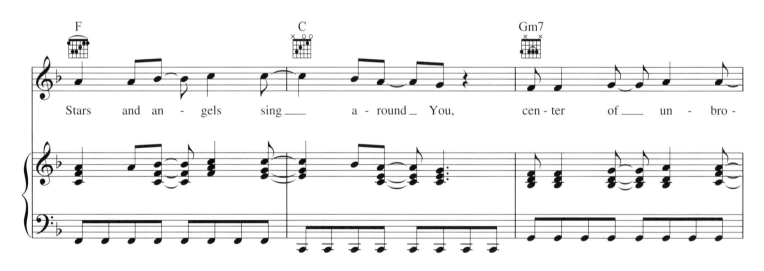

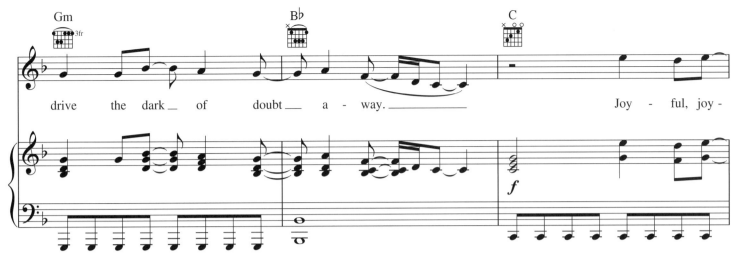

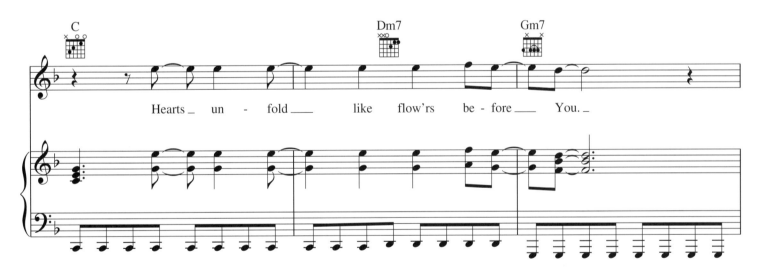

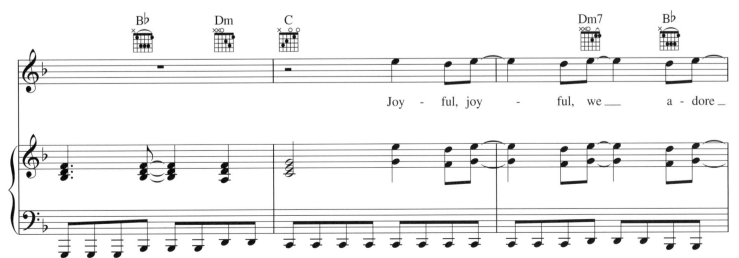

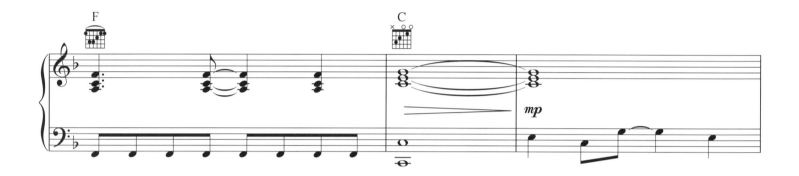

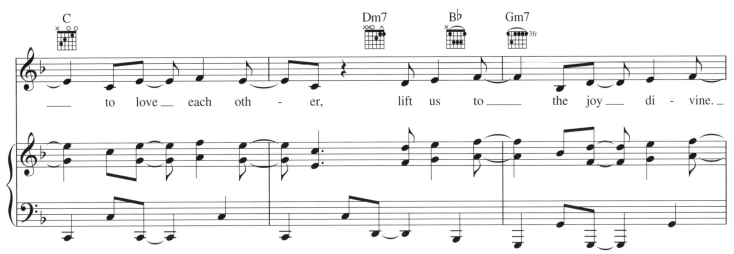

You. ___ Hearts __ un - fold __

___ like flow'rs be - fore ___ You. __ O God, __ our Fa -

- ther, _____ all ___ who live, _____

teach __ us how ___ to love __ each oth - er. _____

AT YOUR FEET

Words and Music by MARK HALL
and JASON INGRAM

Moderate Ballad

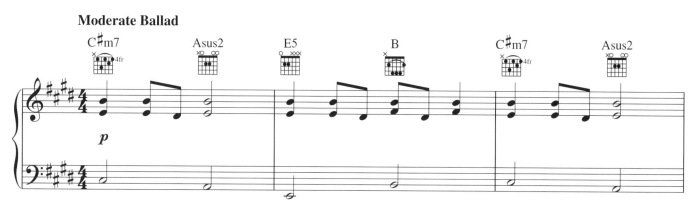

Here at Your feet, I lay my past down,

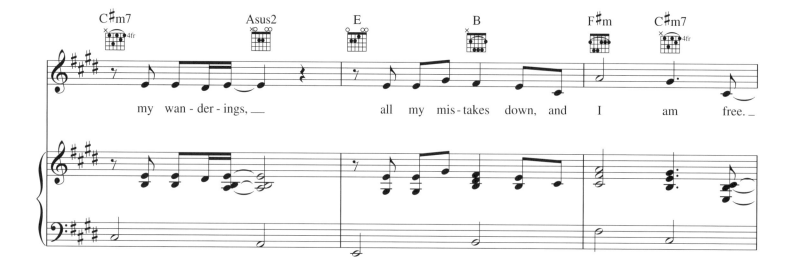

my wan-der-ings, ___ all my mis-takes down, and I am free. ___

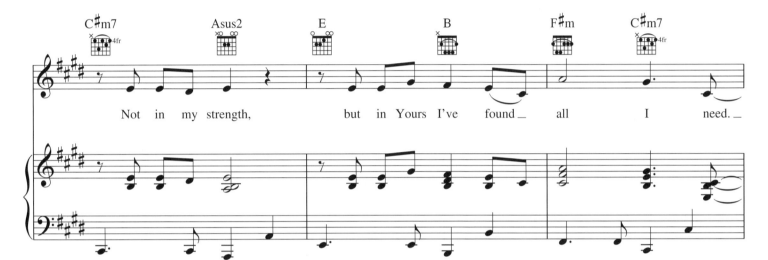

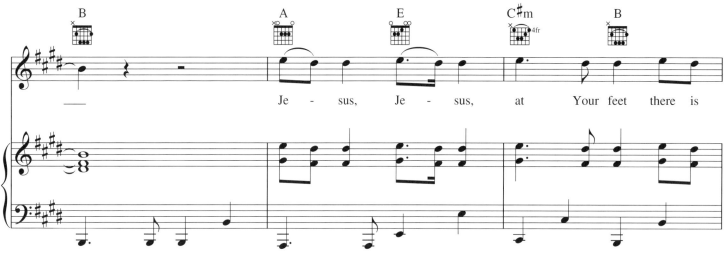

Je - sus, Je - sus, at Your feet there is

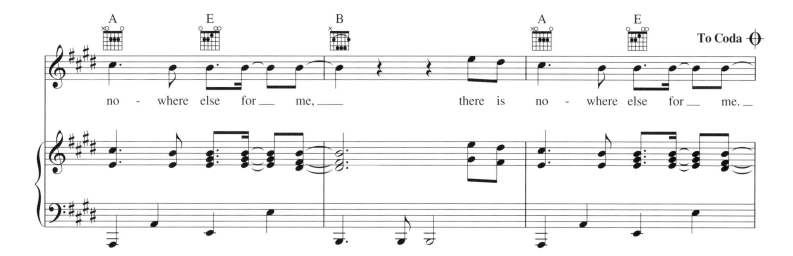

no - where else for __ me, ___ there is no - where else for __ me. __

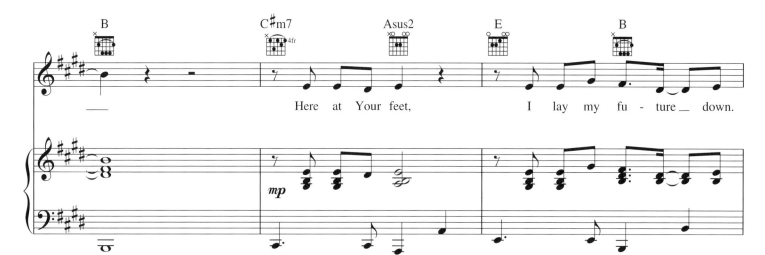

__ Here at Your feet, I lay my fu - ture __ down.

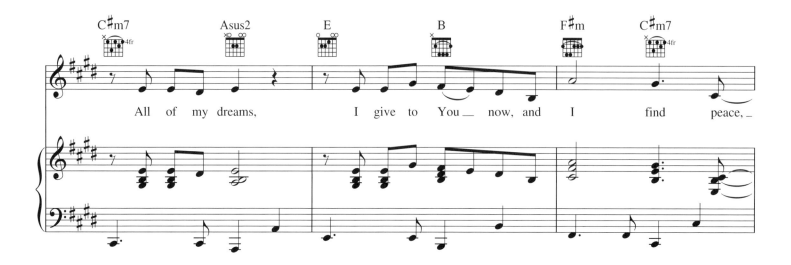

All of my dreams, I give to You __ now, and I find peace, __

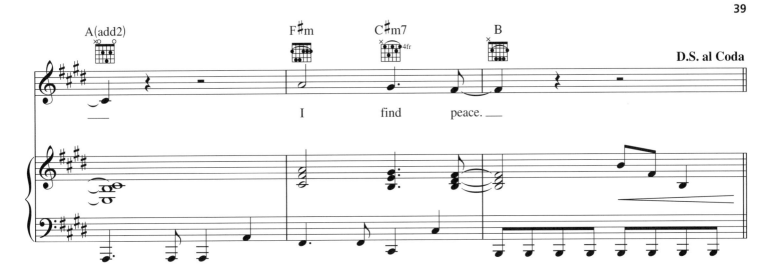

D.S. al Coda

I find peace.

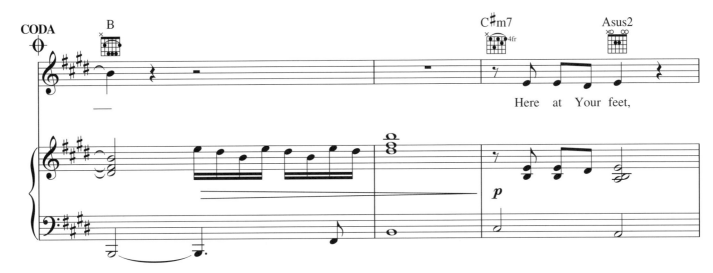

CODA

Here at Your feet,

I lay my life down for You, my King. You're all I want now, and

my soul sings. Je - sus, Je - sus,

at Your feet, oh, to dwell and nev - er ___ leave. ___

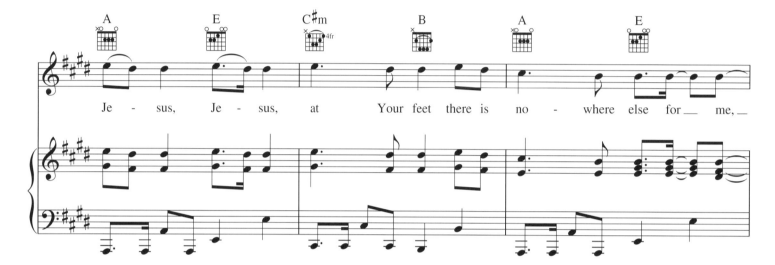

Je - sus, Je - sus, at Your feet there is no - where else for ___ me, ___

___ there is no - where else for ___ me. ___ 'Cause

I ___ am free ___ here at Your ___ feet. All ___ I need ___

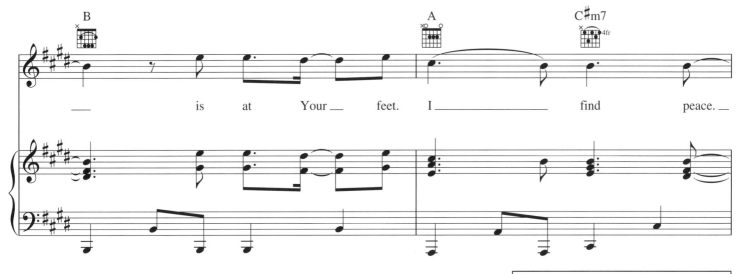

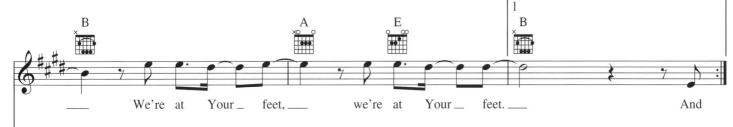

GLORIOUS DAY
(Living He Loved Me)

Words and Music by MARK HALL
and MICHAEL BLEAKER

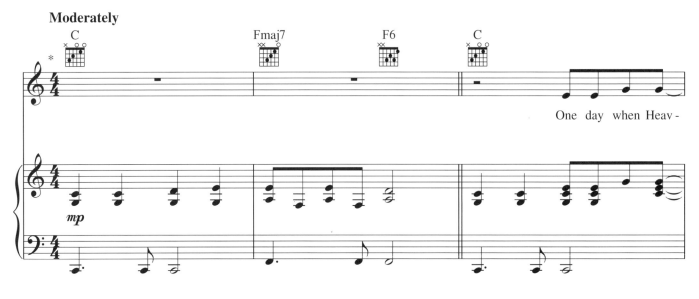

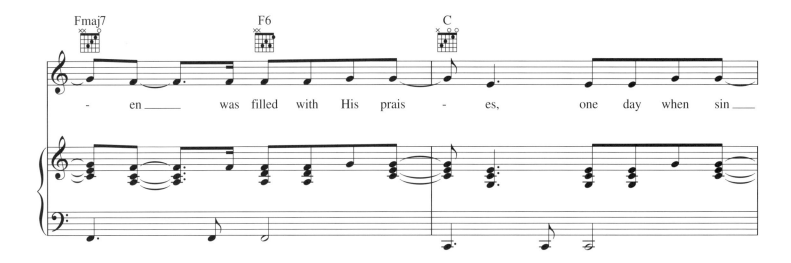

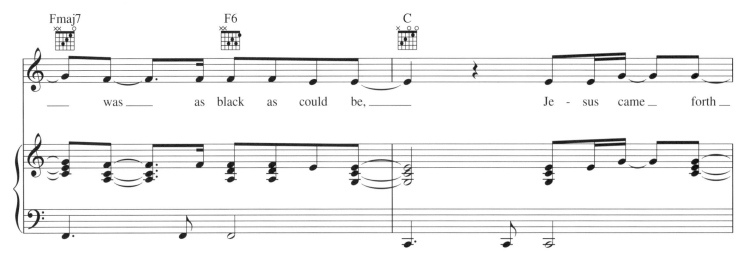

* Recorded a half step lower.

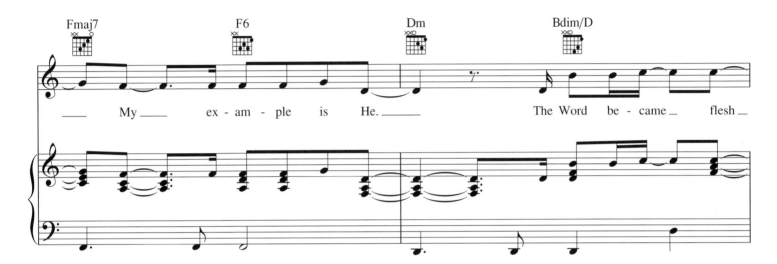

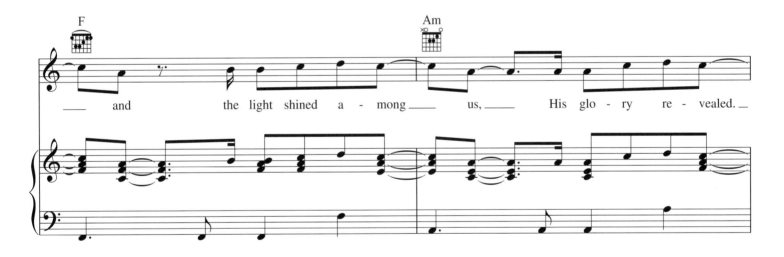

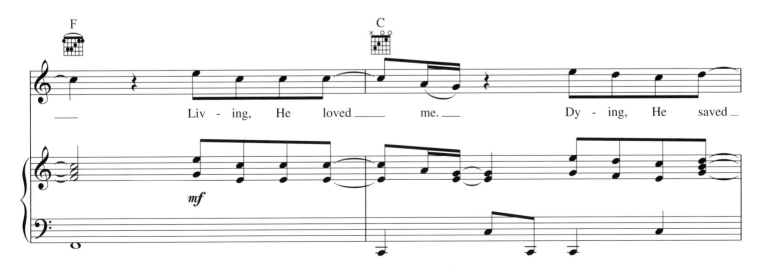

44

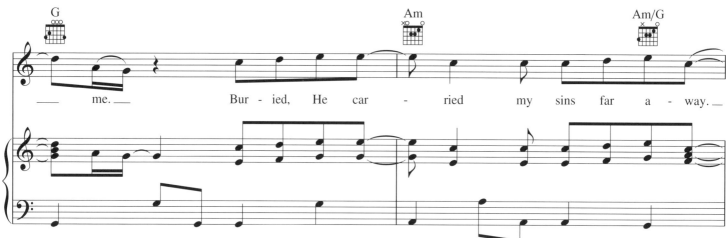

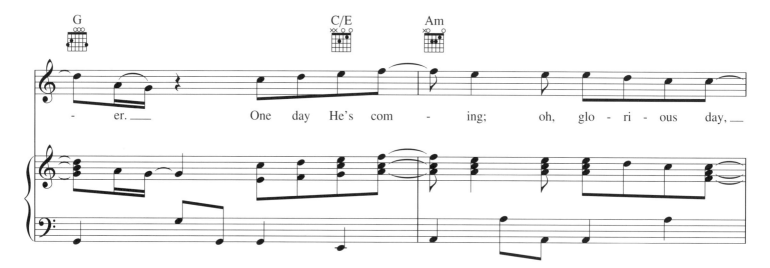

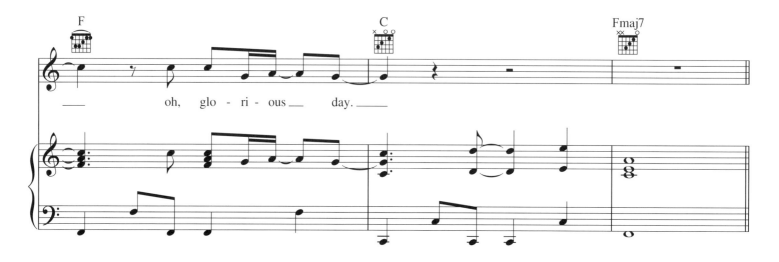

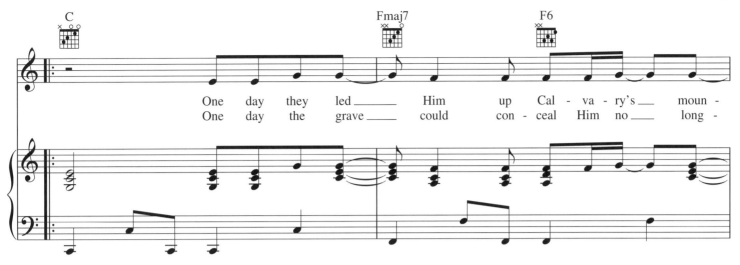

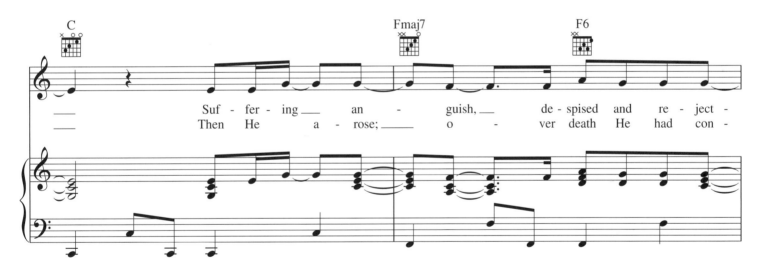

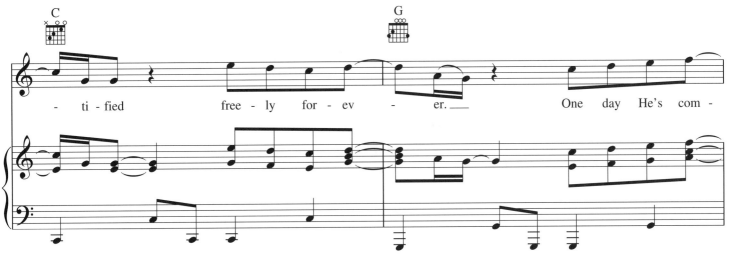

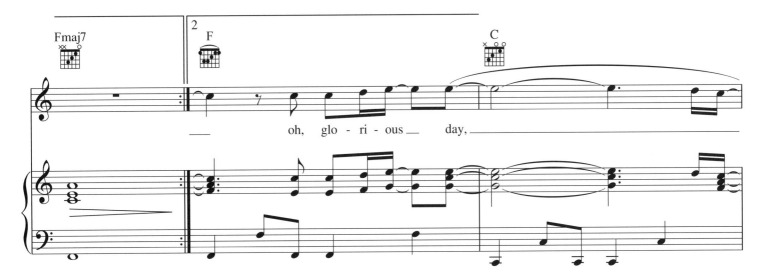

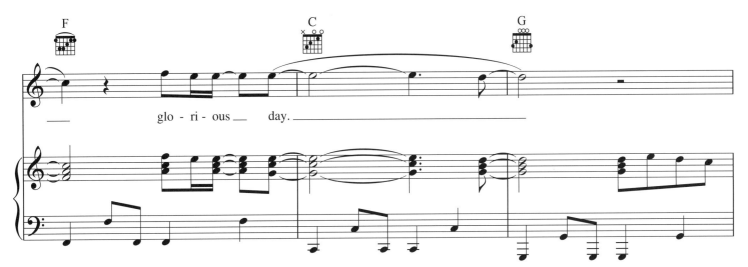

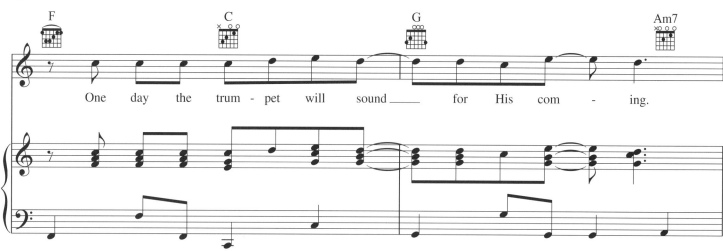

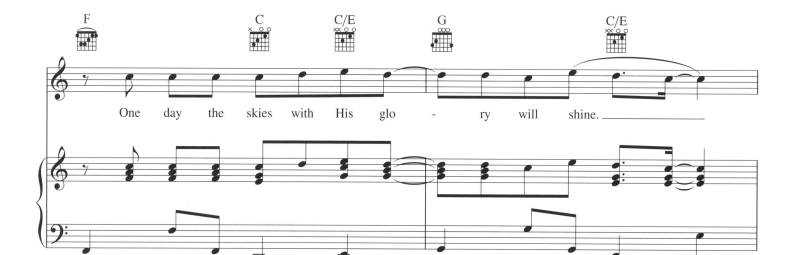

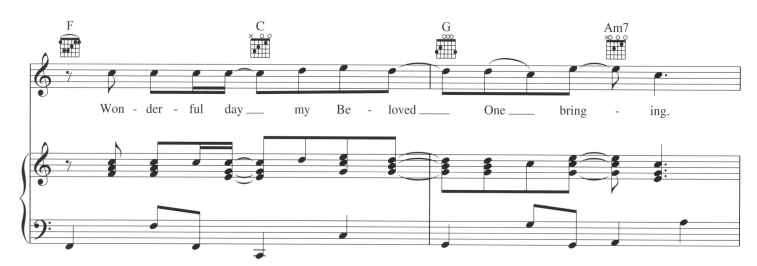

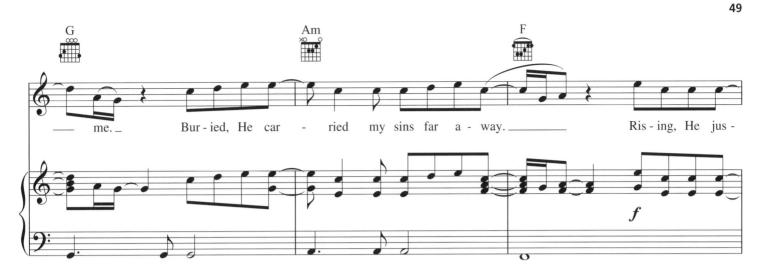

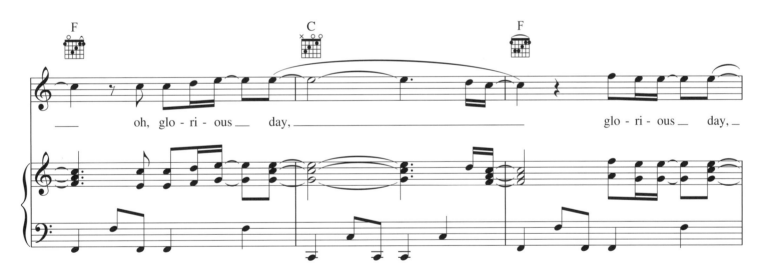

HOLY ONE

Words and Music by MARK HALL,
JASON INGRAM, STUART GARRARD
and MATT BRONLEEWE

Driving Rock beat

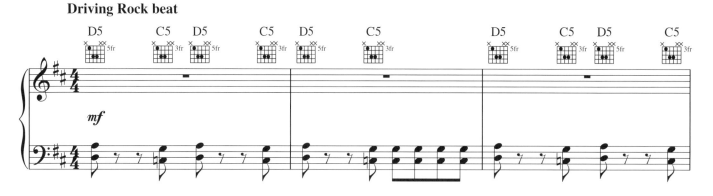

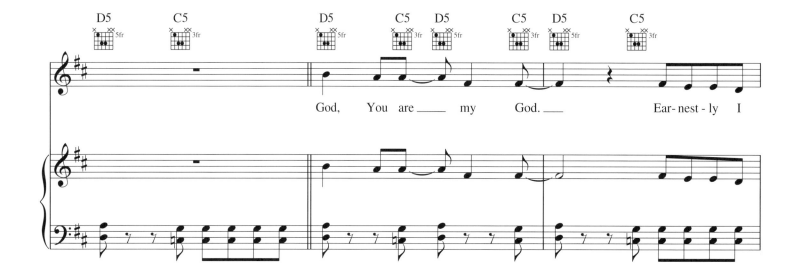

God, You are ___ my God. ___ Ear-nest-ly I

seek You, O ___ my soul. ___ I thirst for You. My bod - y aches ___ in a

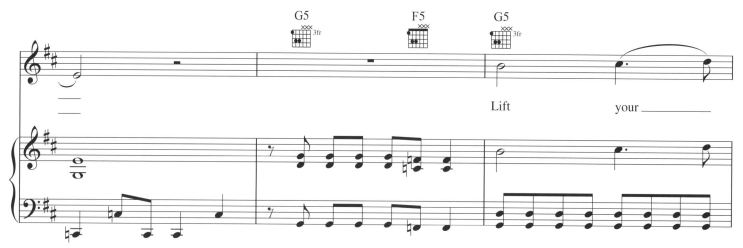

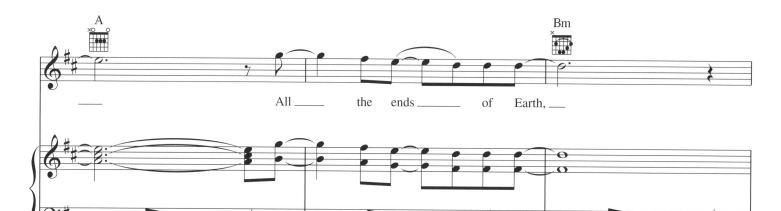

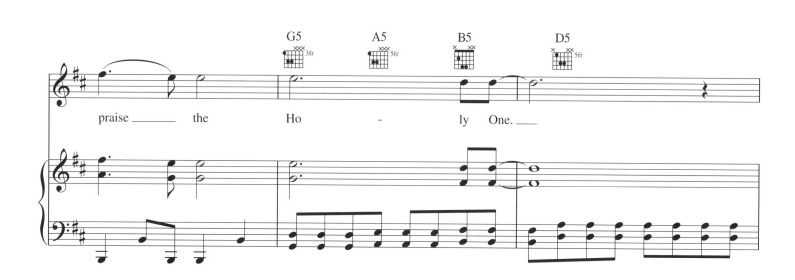

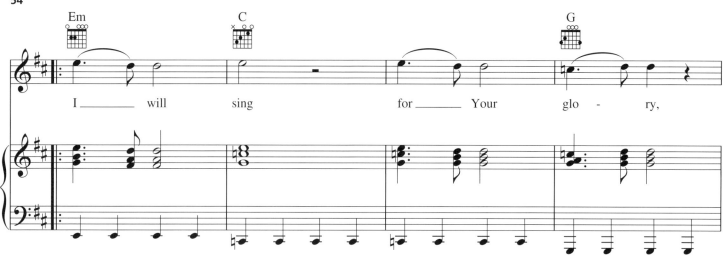

I _____ will sing for _____ Your glo - ry,

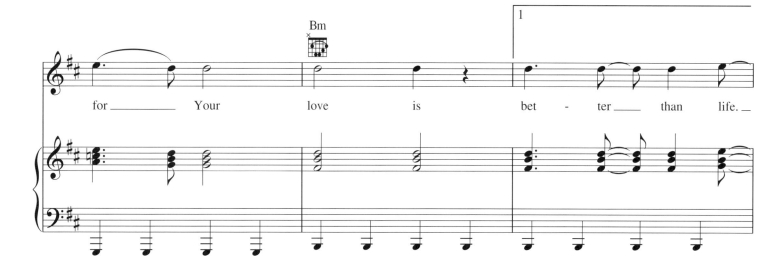

for _____ Your love is bet - ter _____ than life. _____

_____ bet - ter _____ than life, _____

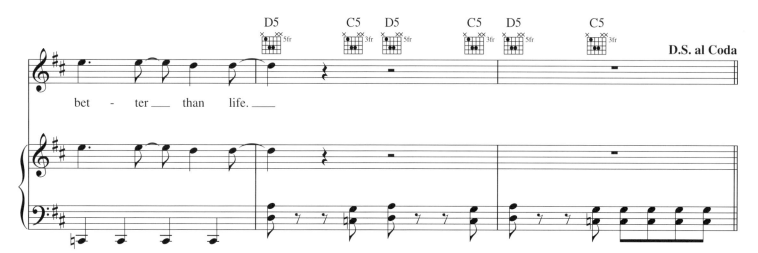

bet - ter _____ than life. _____

D.S. al Coda

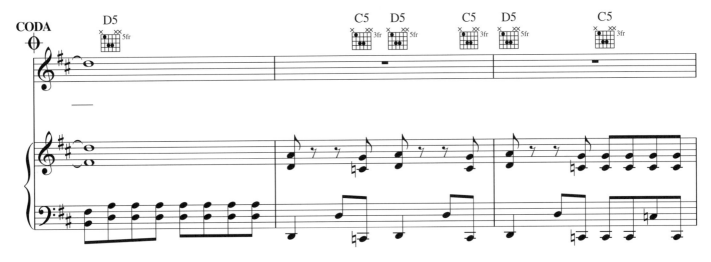

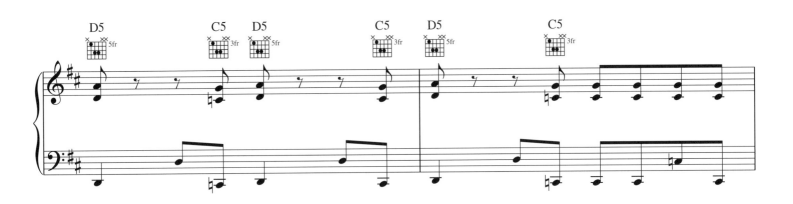

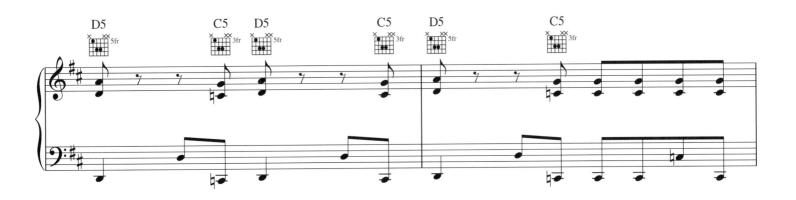

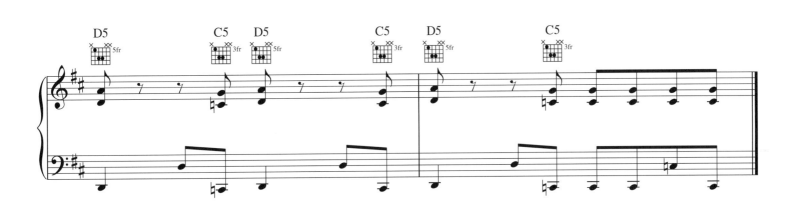

TO KNOW YOU

Words and Music by MARK HALL,
JASON INGRAM and BERNIE HERMS

To know You is to nev-er wor-ry for my life, and

to know You is to nev-er give in or com-pro-mise, and

to know You is to want to tell the world a-bout You,

'cause I _____ can't live with - out _____ You. ___

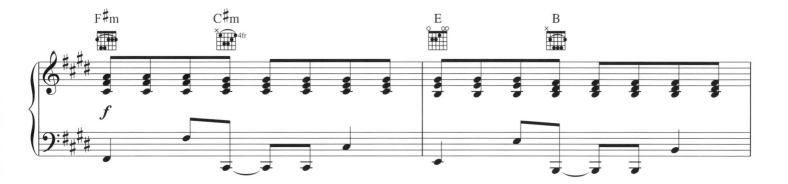

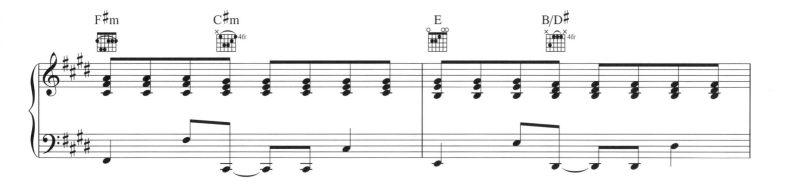

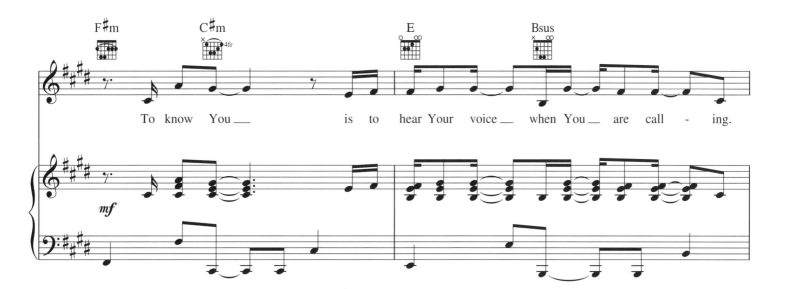

To know You ___ is to hear Your voice ___ when You ___ are call - ing.

To know You ___ is to catch my broth - er when ___ he's fall - ing.

To know You ___ is to feel the pain ___ of the bro - ken - heart - ed,

'cause they ___ can't live with - out ___ You. ___

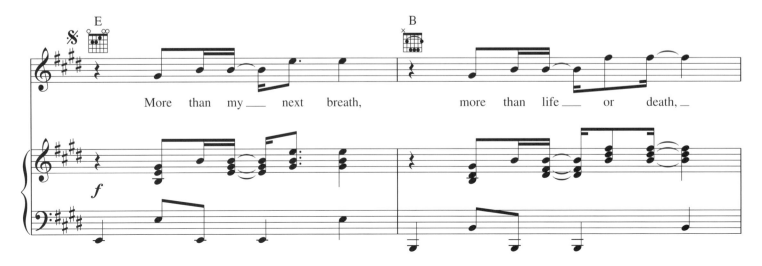

More than my ___ next breath, more than life ___ or death, ___

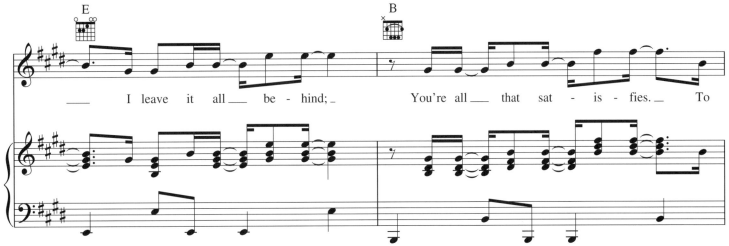

To know You ___ is to ache for more ___ than or - di - nar - y. ___

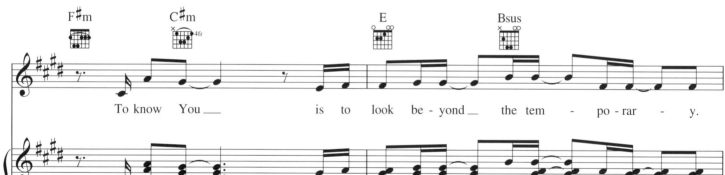

To know You ___ is to look be - yond ___ the tem - po - rar - y.

To know You ___ is be - liev - ing that ___ You'll be ___ e - nough, ___

D.S. al Coda

'cause there's _ no life with - out _____ You. _

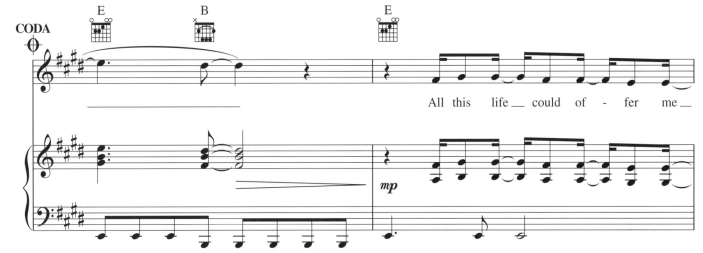

CODA

_____ All this life _ could of - fer me _

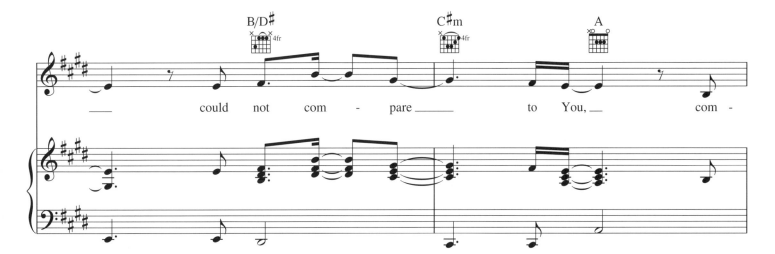

_____ could not com - pare _____ to You, _ com -

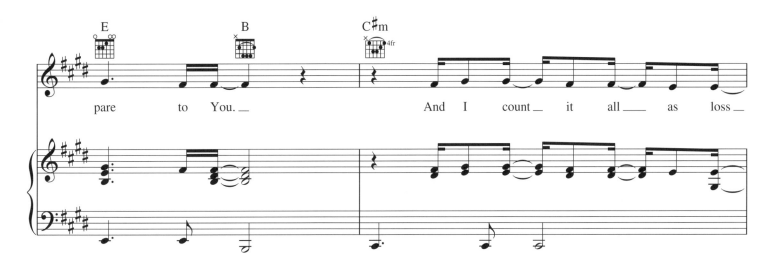

pare to You. _ And I count _ it all _ as loss _

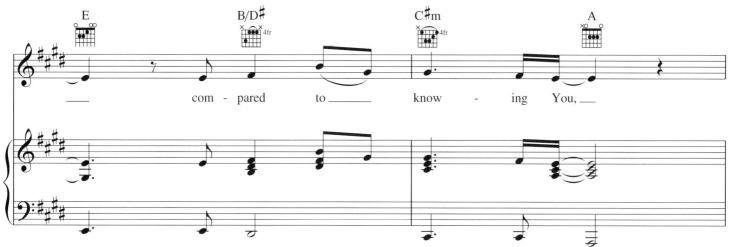

com - pared to _____ know - ing You, _____

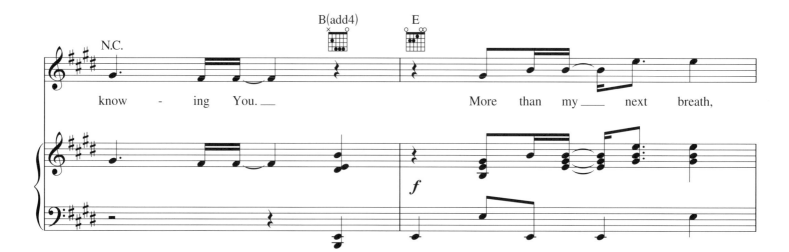

know - ing You. _____ More than my _____ next breath,

more than life _____ or death, _____ all I'm reach - ing for, _____ I

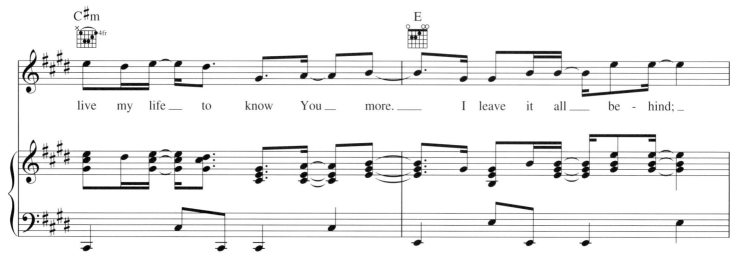

live my life _____ to know You _____ more. _____ I leave it all _____ be - hind; _____

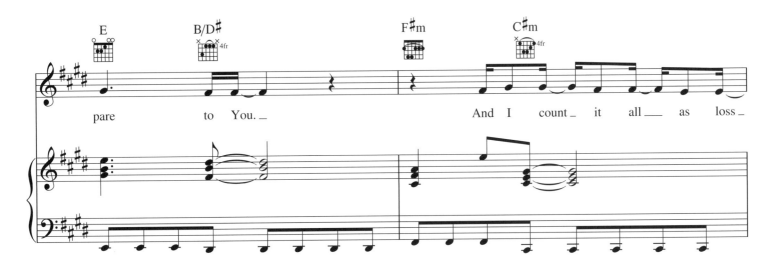

64

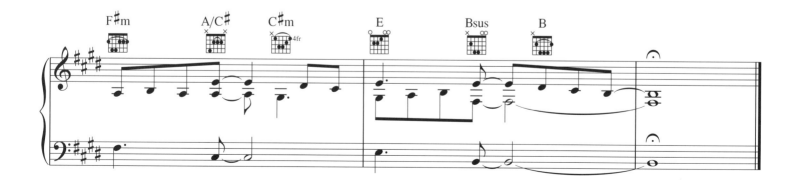

MERCY

Words and Music by MARK HALL,
OMEGA LEVINE, SAM DE LONG
and TAUESE TOFA

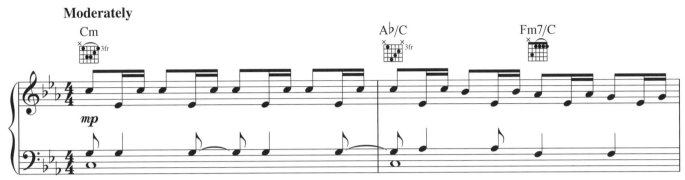

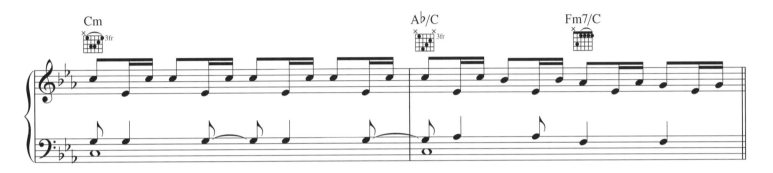

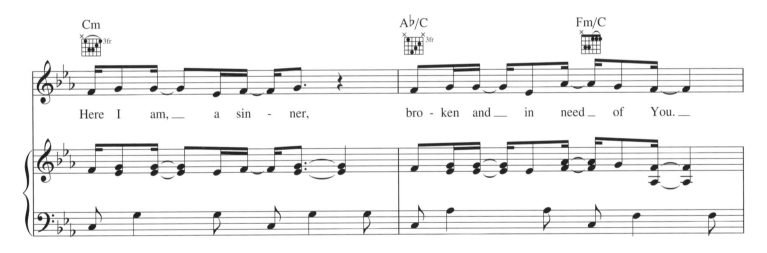

Here I am, a sin - ner, bro - ken and in need of You.

Take my life and wash my fears a - way.

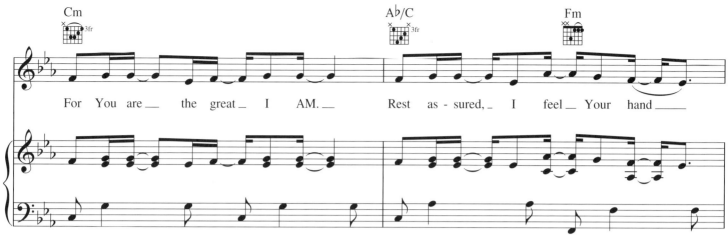

For You are __ the great __ I AM. __ Rest as - sured, __ I feel __ Your hand __

hold - ing me __ un - til __ the dark - ness clears. __ A Fa - ther to __ the fa -

- ther - less, Re - deem - er of __ my soul. __ My life __ is Yours __ for - ev -

- er. My heart will al - ways know __ Your

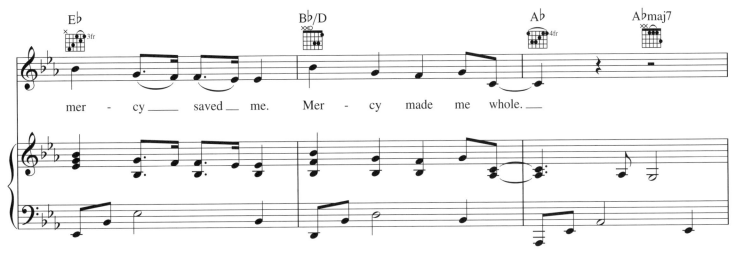

mer - cy____ saved___ me. Mer - cy made me whole.____

Your mer - cy____ found___ me, called____ me as Your own.____

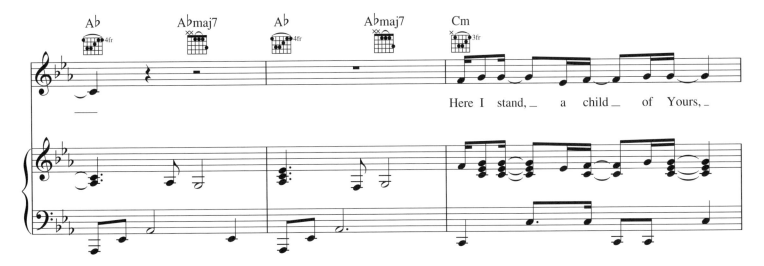

____ Here I stand,___ a child___ of Yours,___

bro - ken and___ in need___ of You.___ Break these chains___ and wash___ my guilt___ a - way.___

Heal - er of __ my bro - ken - ness, _ my

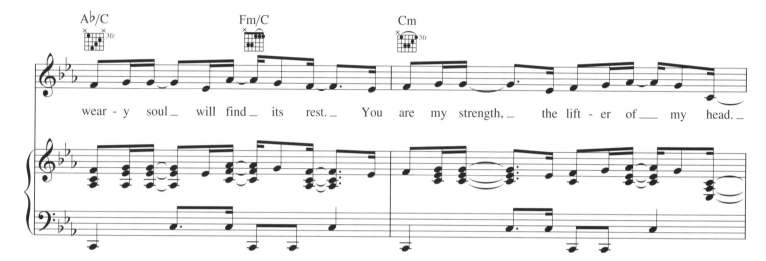

wear - y soul _ will find _ its rest. _ You are my strength, _ the lift - er of __ my head. _

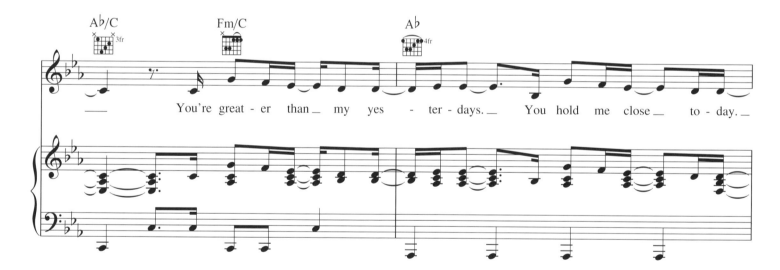

__ You're great - er than _ my yes - ter - days. _ You hold me close _ to - day. _

__ You're the Lord of my _ to - mor - ows. My heart will al - ways say: _

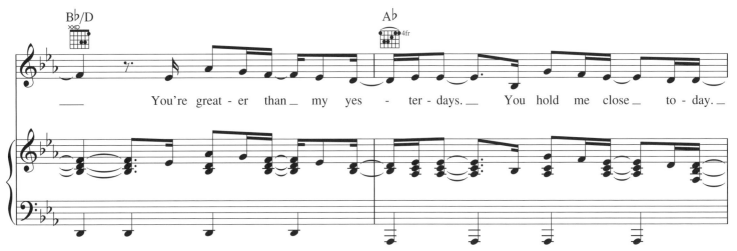

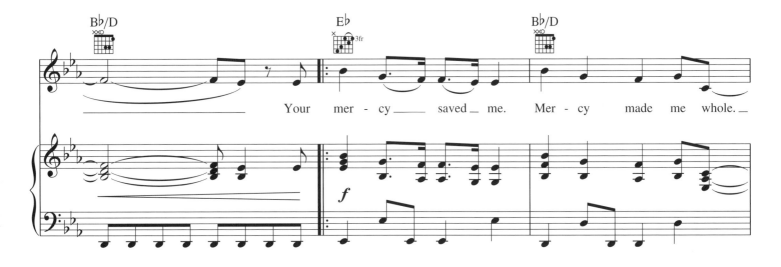

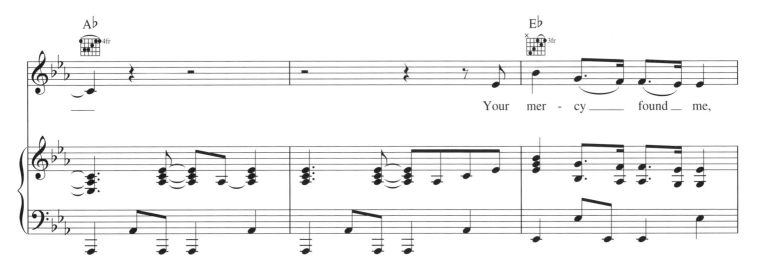

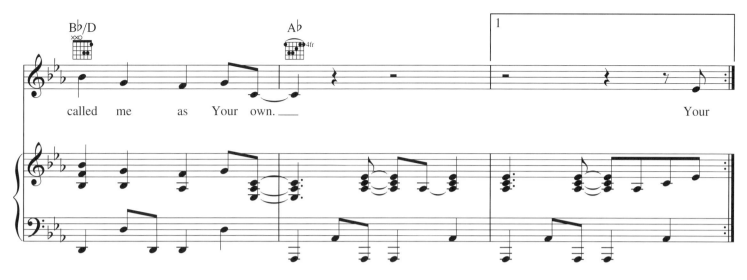

called me as Your own. ____

Your

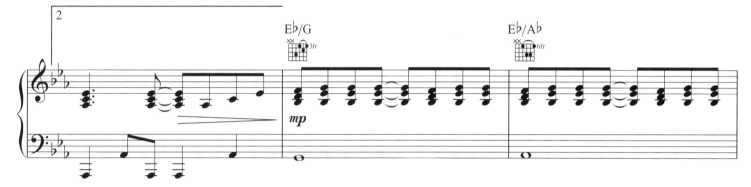

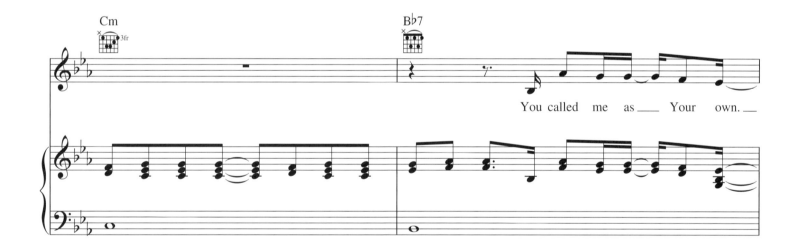

You called me as ____ Your own. ____

_____ You called me as ____ Your own. _____ You called me as ____ Your own. ____

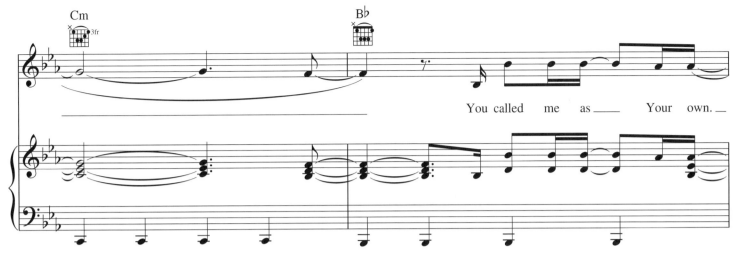

You called me as ___ Your own. ___

You called me as ___ Your own. ___ Called me as ___ Your own. ___

cresc. poco a poco

Thank You for ___ Your mer - cy. ___

___ Thank You for ___ Your mer - cy. ___ Your

mer - cy ____ saved ___ me. Mer - cy made me whole. ____

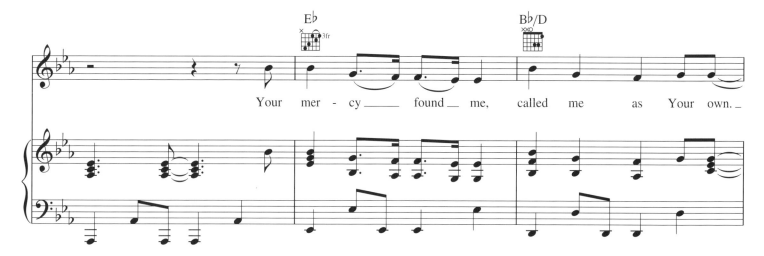

Your mer - cy ____ found ___ me, called me as Your own. ___

_____ Your

You called me as ___ Your own, _

____ Your own. _____

JESUS, HOLD ME NOW

Words and Music by MARK HALL
and BERNIE HERMS

now the storms are clos - ing in, _____ and here I am __ a - gain. _____

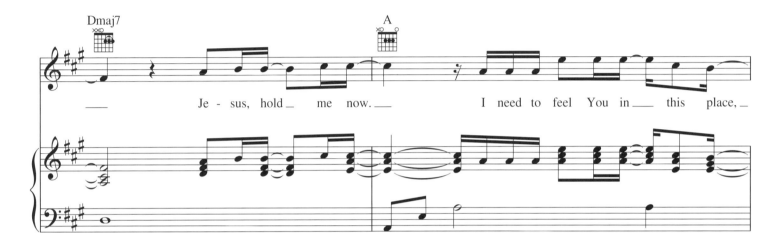

_____ Je - sus, hold __ me now. __ I need to feel You in __ this place,

_____ to know You're by __ my side, __ and hear Your voice __ to - night.

_____ Je - sus, hold __ me now. __ I long for Your __ em - brace.

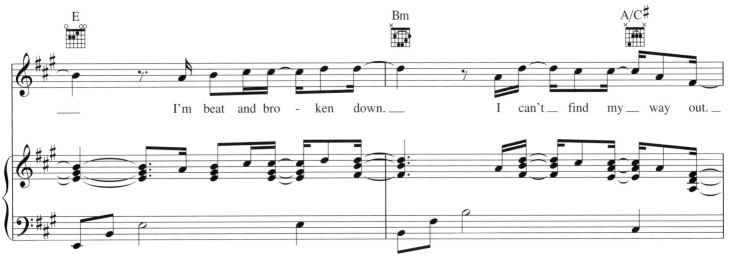

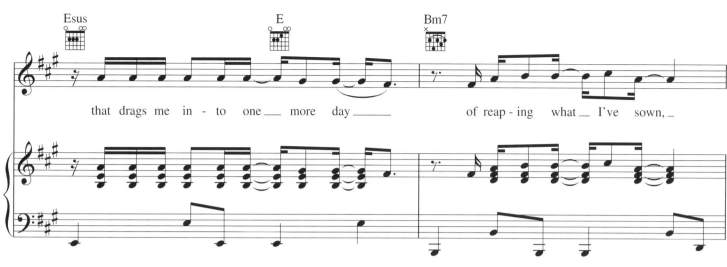

that drags me in - to one __ more day _____ of reap - ing what __ I've sown, _

of liv - ing with __ my shame. ____ So wel - come to __ my world ____

and the life that I ___ have made, ___ where one __ day you're __ a prince, _

—— and the next day you're a slave. _____ Je - sus, hold __ me now. _

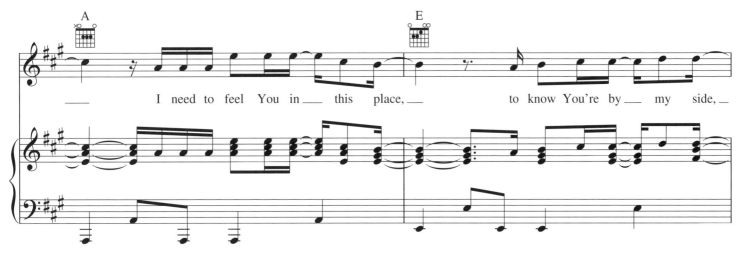

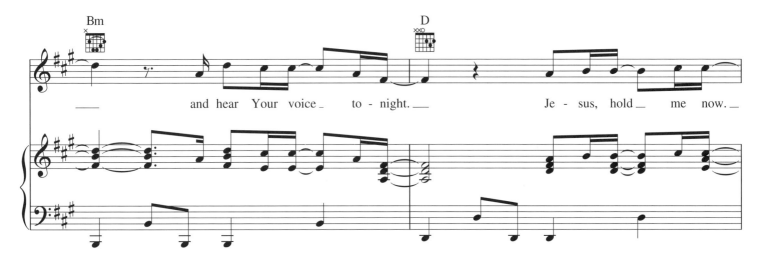

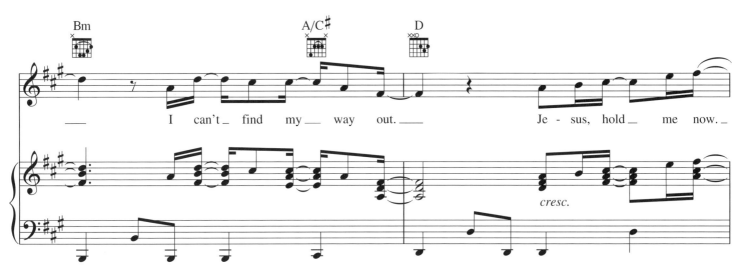

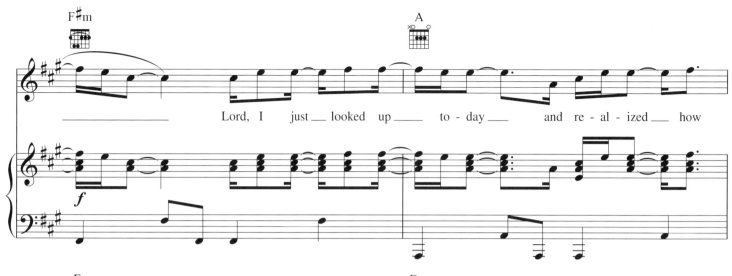

Lord, I just __ looked up __ to - day __ and re - al - ized __ how

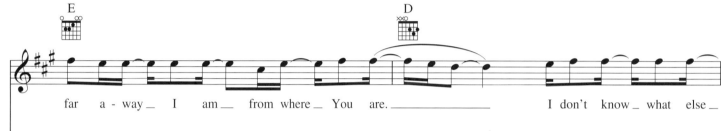

far a - way __ I am __ from where __ You are. _____ I don't know __ what else __

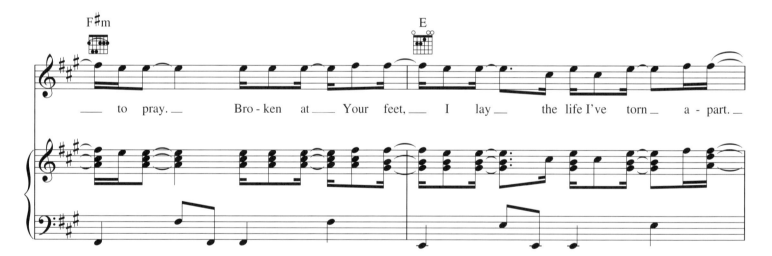

__ to pray. __ Bro - ken at __ Your feet, __ I lay __ the life I've torn __ a - part. __

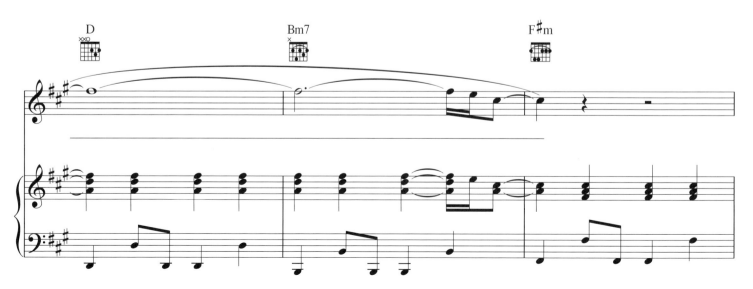

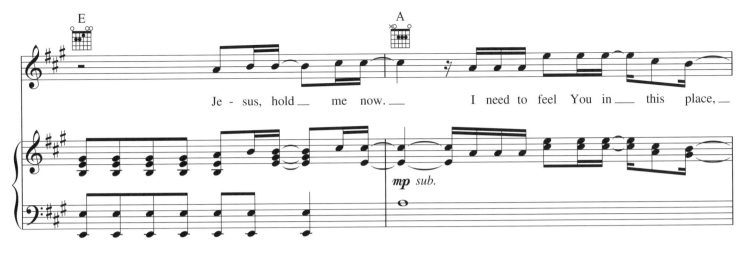

Je - sus, hold __ me now. __ I need to feel You in __ this place, __

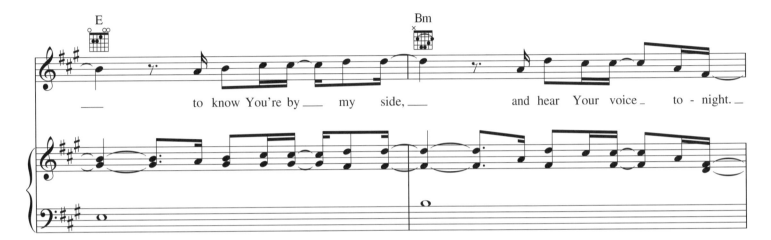

__ to know You're by __ my side, __ and hear Your voice __ to - night. __

__ Je - sus, hold __ me now. __ I long for Your __ em - brace. __

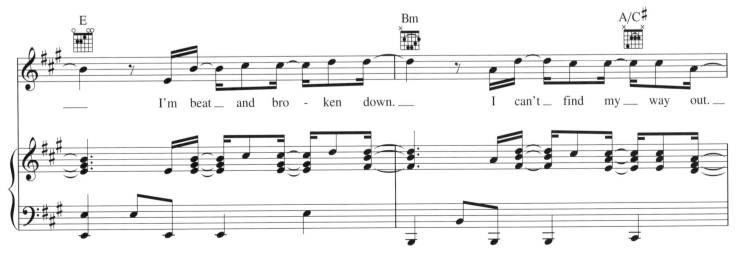

__ I'm beat __ and bro - ken down. __ I can't __ find my __ way out. __

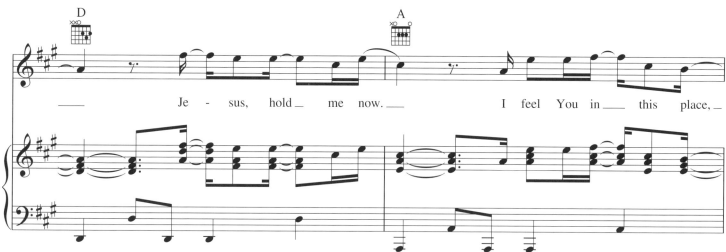

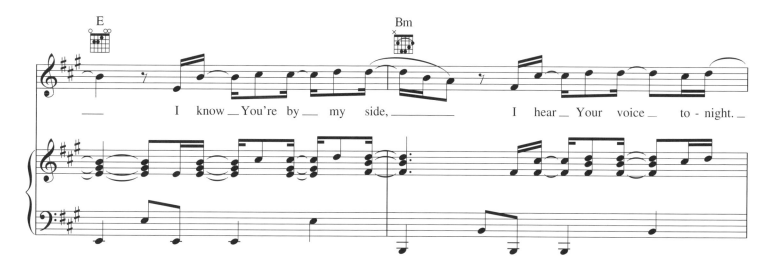

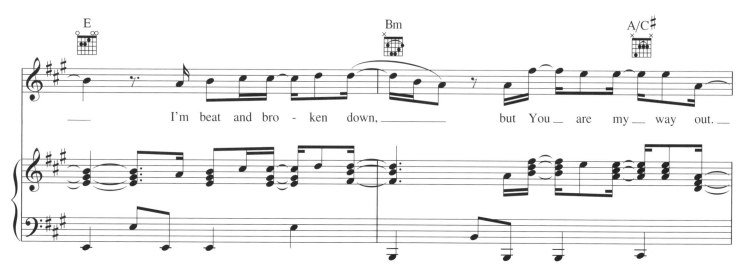

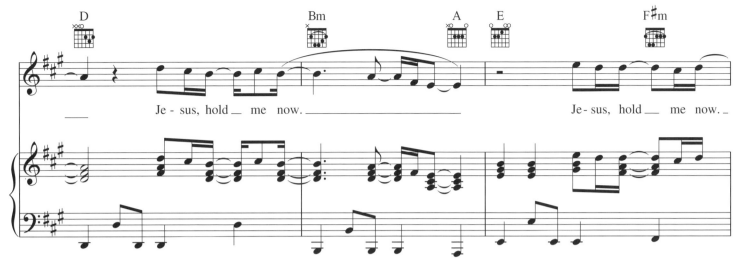

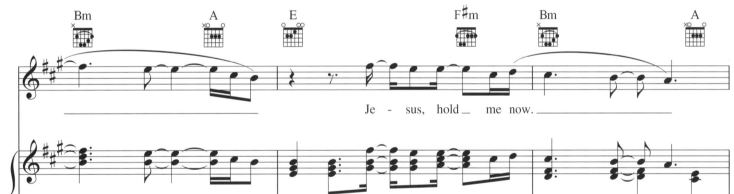

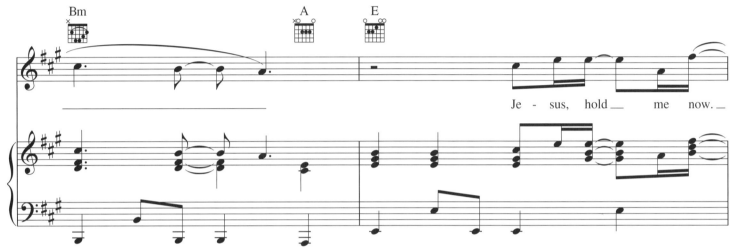

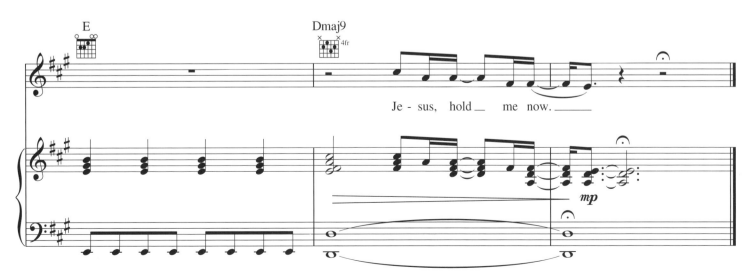

BLESSED REDEEMER

Words and Music by MARK HALL
and BERNIE HERMS

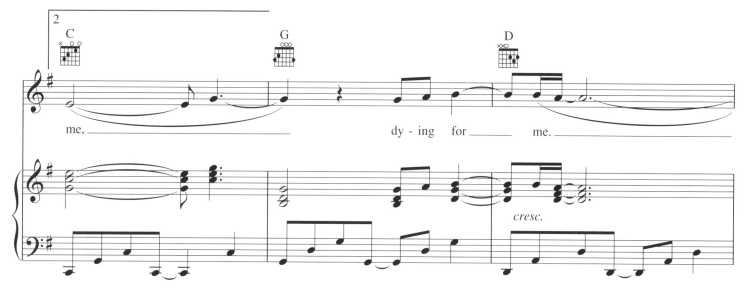

me, _____ dy - ing for _____ me. _____

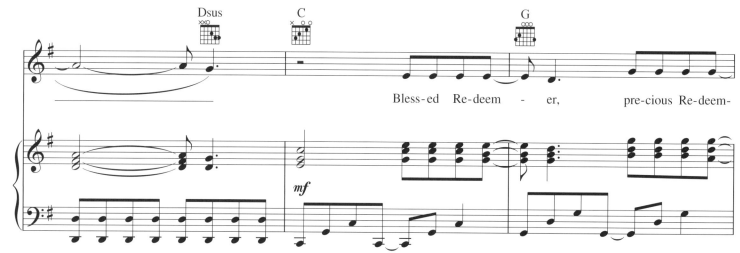

_____ Bless-ed Re-deem - er, pre-cious Re-deem-

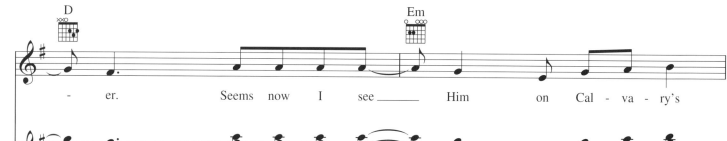

- er. Seems now I see _____ Him on Cal - va - ry's

tree. _____ Wound-ed and bleed - ing, for sin-ners plead-

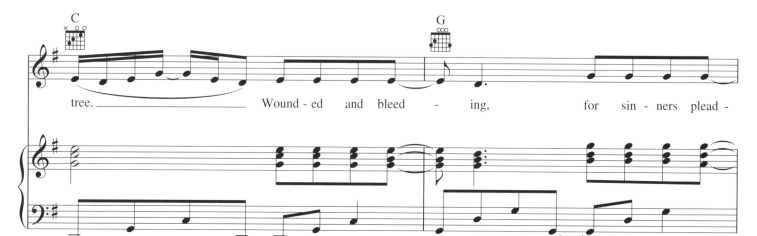

-ing, blind and un-heed - ing, dy - ing for

me. _____ Oh, how _ I love _

___ Him, Sav-ior and Friend. _ How can _ my prais - es ev - er find end? _

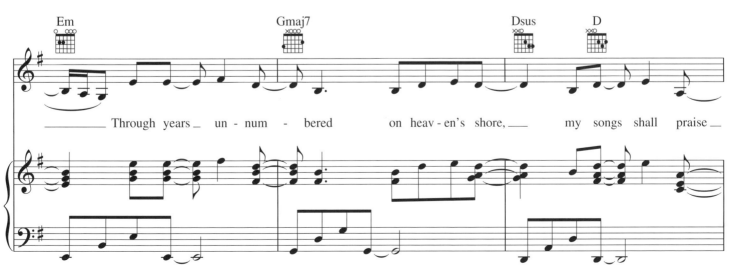

_____ Through years _ un - num - bered on heav-en's shore, ___ my songs shall praise _

Him for - ev - er - more. _____ Bless - ed Re - deem - er, pre - cious Re - deem -

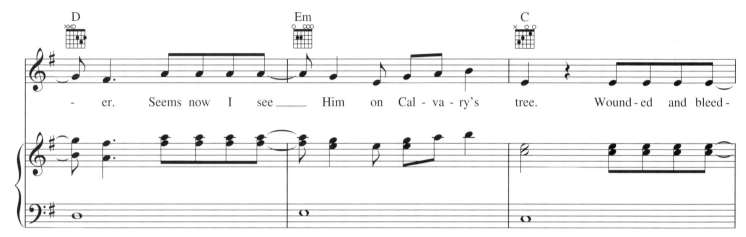

- er. Seems now I see _____ Him on Cal - va - ry's tree. Wound - ed and bleed -

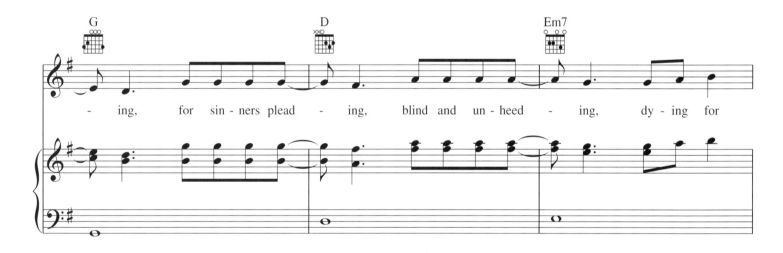

- ing, for sin - ners plead - ing, blind and un - heed - ing, dy - ing for

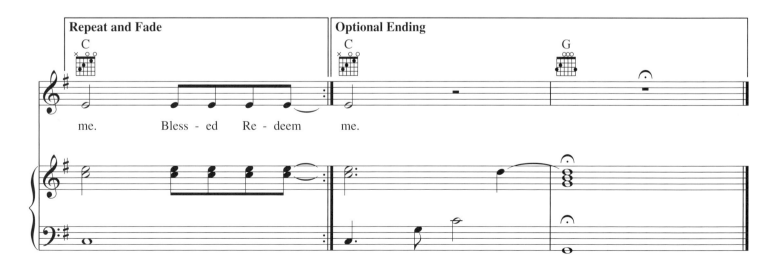

Repeat and Fade

me. Bless - ed Re - deem me.

Optional Ending

me.